The Lay: Understa: Statements

1

How to Read, Analyze, Create & Understand Balance Sheets, Income Statements, Cash Flow & More

By

Simon J. Lawrence

Lost River
Publishing House

Cover design

Lisa Cunningham

First Edition

Contents

3

Introduction

When I started my first business, I had no idea that I would have to interpret financial statements or even prepare them. However, it was not long before the bills started piling up. I found myself mixing my revenue with my personal finances, and I couldn't track my profits. It was at this point that I realized I needed to invest in financial management. I hired a bookkeeper with the hope of getting everything sorted out. In less than three months, I realized that my bookkeeper was keeping my money instead of the books. Long story short, I learned a valuable lesson from my initial mistakes in business.

No matter how well your business is operating, you must be able to manage your finances if you want it to have a future. I did not have to attend accounting school; however, I have learned how to manage my accounts books, process taxes, and payroll, among others.

For any person getting into business, financial management is an area of interest. If you are a manager or a business owner, your main duty is to monitor the flow of finances, plan for the daily operations of the business, and invest in the future of the business. You cannot achieve any of these objectives unless you can interpret your financial statements and maintain your books of accounts well. If you are not able to read and interpret your financial statements, most of the accountants you hire may take advantage of the situation to mismanage the funds.

In this book, I will be helping you learn how to keep your books, prepare financial statements, and interpret them. These are the key areas of accounting that you must pay attention to if you wish to manage your finances. The main area of concern for most accountants is interpreting financial statements. In this book, we will be helping you learn how to interpret your financial statements and make the best out of them.

To ensure that you gain the most from this book, I have broken it into sections that are simple to understand. Each section builds up from the known towards the unknown. In the first section of the book, we start by introducing you to the general bookkeeping and accounting principles. Given that this book is based on the American accounting system, it will help you learn what you need to know when managing your business in the US. In the introductory section, we help you understand the importance of accounting and the reason why you need to invest in accounting.

In the second section of the book, we introduce you to the more technical aspects of accounting, in the most simplified way. When I started my first business, I tried reading many accounting books, but I could not understand anything. From my personal experience, I have made it my mission to make accounting as simple as possible. In this section, I will introduce you to financial statements in the most simplistic way possible. You do not have to be an accountant to understand or prepare financial statements. I will help you prepare all the major financial statements from scratch. I will show you short cut methods that you can use to verify the figures being provided by your accountants and the best ways to ensure that your finances are adding up.

In the third section of the book, we focus on interpreting and benefiting the most from financial statements. Probably, you do not want to prepare financial statements, but you wish to interpret them. In this section, I will break it down to you in the simplest way possible. As long as you can account for your personal finances, managing, and accounting for your business, finances will not be a problem. I will help you learn how to track down your expenses, revenue, assets, capital, and the growth of your business.

In the fourth section of the book, we look at some of the common errors that individuals make in day to day accounting. If you are not an accounting expert, you might end up making mistakes that are costly. We are going to look at some of the mistakes that you must avoid. If you are hiring accountants, we will help you know the questions to ask and the approach to take to ensure that there is transparency.

If you are a business owner, a manager, or an aspiring business owner, this book is for you. This is not an accounting educational paper, but rather a guide that simplifies accounting to the average person. Even if you did not attend formal school, this book will help you manage the finances of your business, seal all possible loopholes, and ensure that your business grows.

Throughout this book, we have used examples, illustrations,

and diagrams that will help simplify your work. By reading through the book once, you should be able to handle basic bookkeeping and accounting tasks. Welcome aboard, and enjoy your reading.

Chapter 1: Accounting and Bookkeeping Principles

Accounting is a broad subject that you cannot master in a few days. However, you can master the basics of accounting and be able to start taking care of your business accounts in just a week. The aim of this book is not to make you a professional accountant but rather, to help you manage your accounts without necessarily depending on anyone. To be able to become an accountant in such a short period of time, you will have to focus on the key principles of the subject. In this chapter, I am going to introduce you to the key principles of accounting and bookkeeping. I will help you understand what accounting really is, how different it is from bookkeeping, and how to manage your books, among other factors. However, before we even start looking at what accounting is, we should define some of the terms that are commonly used by accountants. You will encounter most of these terms throughout the book. It is in your best interest to keep them at the back of your mind so as to make your understanding of the book much easier.

Defining Terminology

Accounts Receivable (AR): The accounts receivable is an entry in the books of accounts that represents the money or assets owned by customers or clients. Think of accounts receivable as money that belongs to the business but is currently in the hands of another party.

Accounting (ACCG): The abbreviation ACCG is used to refer to accounting, which stands for a systematic way of recording and reporting financial transactions of a business entity. The term accounting is only used for established businesses that can sue or be sued.

Accounts Payable (AP): Accounts payable is the opposite of accounts receivable. The accounts payable is an entry in the books of accounts that represents the money your business owes creditors such as suppliers. If you purchase goods and services on credit, you should record the amount to be paid within the accounts payable.

Assets (fixed and current) (FA, CA): The term assets is used to refer to all the items of value that are owned by the company. If you are running a business, anything that adds value to your business can be referred to as an asset. Assets are divided into Current Assets CA and Fixed Assets FA. Current assets refer to the valuable items that will be converted to cash within one year. They include things such as cash, inventory, accounts, receivable, etc. Fixed assets, on the other hand, refers to assets that cannot be converted into cash within a year. Examples of fixed assets include machinery, real estate, land, etc.

Asset Classes: The term asset classes is used to refer to a group of securities that behave in a similar way in the marketplace. The main asset classes are equities, fixed income bonds, and cash equivalents.

Balance Sheet (BS): A balance sheet is one of the major financial statements prepared by accountants. It is a report that summarizes the company's assets, liabilities, and owner's equity within a given time. It is through the balance sheet that you are able to determine the growth of your business over the years.

Capital (CAP): The term capital is used to refer to the money or assets that the company can put into use. Working capital refers to the money that is currently available for the operations of the business. Working capital is calculated by subtracting current liabilities from Current assets.

Cash Flow (CF): The term cash flow literally means the flow of cash in your business. It is used to mean the revenue or expenses expected to be generated through business activities such as manufacturing, sales, procurement, etc. Cash flow statements are prepared within a given period of time.

Certified Public Accountant (CPA): The term certified public accountant is used when referring to an individual who has passed the standardized CPA exam and attained the required work experience. In other words, to become a CPA, you must meet certain terms, which include passing the exam and gaining work experience. The good news is that you do not have to pass any exams to become an accountant at your business.

Cost of Goods Sold (COGS): The cost of goods sold refers to the direct expenses related to the goods sold by a business. The cost of goods sold can be arrived at by using different formulas depending on the business model. For instance, the cost of goods sold in the retail business is as simple as the cost of purchasing the goods from the supplier. However, in a manufacturing business, the cost of goods sold might include the cost of raw material, labor, and power, among other factors.

Credit (CR): The word credit, as used in accounting, refers to an entry in the books of accounts that indicates a decrease in assets or an increase in liabilities and equity on a balance sheet. As we will see later, if you are using a double-entry method of bookkeeping, every transaction recorded must have two entries (A debit and a credit entry).

Debit (DR): The term debit is the opposite of credit. A debit is an entry into the books of accounting that indicates either an increase in assets or a decrease in liabilities on the balance sheet.

Diversification: This refers to the process of allocating capital to various assets. In diversification, a company might choose to invest in different areas from its main operations in a bid to reduce risks

Enrolled Agent (EA): An enrolled agent is a tax expert who represents taxpayers when dealing with the Internal Revenue Authorities. You may hire an enrolled agent to help you process your taxes, or you may choose to process taxes yourself.

Expenses (fixed, variable, accrued, operation): The term expenses is used to refer to the amount of money used on a day to day business operations. There are 4 main types of expenses. We have fixed expenses (FE), which refers to payments such as rent that will happen regularly, whether the business is operational or not. Variable expenses (VE) represent expenditures such as labor that may change over a given period. We have accrued expenses (AE), which represent expenses that are yet to be paid. Lastly, we have operational expenses, which include expenses that are not directly related to the production of goods or services such as taxes, insurance, etc.

Equity and Owner's Equity (OE): In the simplest terms possible, equity refers to assets minus liabilities. The remaining value after subtracting liabilities from companies' assets is what we call equity; in other words, the portion of the company that is owned by the shareholders of the business. Owners' equity is defined as the percentage of stock a person has an ownership interest in the company.

Insolvency: A company can be declared insolvent if it cannot meet its debt obligations. A company that is insolvent has a negative owner's equity, in that the assets of the company are way lesser than the liabilities.

Generally Accepted Accounting Principles (GAAP): The GAAPs are just a set of rules that govern accountants and businesses. These rules are in place to ensure that there is coherence between financial reports produced by different businesses. Following the GAAPs is compulsory for all businesses but very crucial for publicly traded companies.

General Ledger (GL): The general ledger is an important book of accounting that presents a complete record of the financial transactions of a business over its life. When transactions are accurately recorded in specialty ledgers, the transactions are then summarized in the general ledger. For a business to have successful financial management, it must keep an accurate general ledger.

Trial Balance: A trial balance is a financial statement prepared by the contents of a general ledger. All the transactions in the general ledger are compiled into debit and credits to ensure that the company's bookkeeping system works. At any period of compilation, the credit and debit transactions of a business must balance. If the trial balance does not balance, chances are that there are transactions that have been mined or inaccurately entered.

Liabilities (current and long-term): The term liability is used to refer to all the debts a company incurred during business operations. Liabilities are divided into the current and long term. Current liabilities (CL) refer to the debts of a business that must be paid within 1 year, such as debts to suppliers. Long term liabilities (LTL) refer to debts of the company that can be paid over a longer period exceeding one year. An example of a long term liability is a long term mortgage loan.

Limited Liability Company (LLC): A limited liability company is a structure of business where the owners of the company cannot be held liable for the company's debts and liabilities. This type of business shields the owners from losing personal properties in case the business becomes insolvent.

Net Income (NI): The net income of a company NI refers to the total earnings over a given trading period calculated by subtracting expenses from total revenue.

Present Value (PV): The term present value is used to refer to the current value of a future sum of money. For example, if I told you I will give you $100 next year, or I give you $100 now, you will see the money being given now more valuable than the same amount 1 year later. If this money is owed to you, it must accumulate interest over the years to meet the current value 1 year later. Since money at hand has the ability to be invested and multiply, the present value helps us determine the value of cash in the future.

Profit and Loss Statement (P&L): The profit and loss statement is one of the most important financial statements. This statement is used to summarize a company's performance by reviewing revenues, expenses, and costs over a given trading period.

Return on Investment (ROI): Return on investment as a measure used to evaluate the performance of a business relative to the money invested. For instance, if you were to invest $1000 today in a business that generates $2000 in 1 year, your return on the same investment will be $1000. The return on investment helps us determine whether an investment is viable or not. The ROI is calculated by dividing net profit by the cost of investment.

Individual Retirement Account (IRA, Roth IRA): The term IRA is used to refer to a retirement savings plan. A traditional IRA arrangement allows employees to direct untaxed funds towards an investment that grows with deferred taxes. In IRAs, the tax obligation is just deferred but not neglected. Roth is a type of retirement investment vehicle where tax is not deferred. In other words, the eligible distributions are tax-free.

401K & Roth 401K: The 401K is a type of retirement savings vehicle that allows an individual to direct part of their compensation into an investment-based retirement account. The money deferred will not be subjected to taxation until time for withdrawal. However, any member with Roth 401K can still make contributions after taxes, which eliminates the need for taxation at the time of withdrawal.

Subchapter S Corporation (S-CORP): An S-Corp is a type of corporation that meets specific IRS requirements. Such corporations are taxed as partnerships as opposed to being taxed as corporations. Publicly traded companies are subject to double taxation of dividends, something that is exempted from the S-Corps.

Bonds and Coupons (B&C): A bond is a type of debt investment referred to as fixed security. A bond refers to when an investor, be it an individual, a company, or a local government, loans money to another entity with the promise of receiving the money back with interest. For all bonds, there is an annual interest that is paid. The annual interest paid on top of the bond is what we refer to as a coupon.

Retained Earnings (RE): Retained earnings refer to the profits of a business that are plowed back into the company after paying taxes and dividends. When a company makes profits, some of the money has to go into paying liabilities and paying dividends to shareholders. The money that remains and is retained in the business is referred to as retained earnings.

What are Accounting and Bookkeeping

Accounting is the process of consolidating, summarizing, analyzing, and reporting financial records of a company. An accountant is responsible for ensuring that financial reports are prepared and analyzed accordingly. An accountant is also consulted in regard to interpreting and explaining the accounting records. On the other hand, bookkeeping is the practice of recording all the process of accounting.

A bookkeeper is an individual who is basically hired to maintain the database. Every transaction that takes place in a company must be recorded for future reference and proper accounting. It is the work of a bookkeeper to record and organize the transactions of a company. In general terms, both bookkeeping and accounting can be done by an accountant. The bookkeeper only comes into the picture to reduce the workload for the accountant. Essentially, all the work done by a bookkeeper can be done by an accountant effectively. However, since most businesses have so many transactions, they leave the task of recording transactions to bookkeepers and hand the task of analyzing the financial performance of a business to the accountant.

Although accountants and bookkeepers perform very different roles, they are complementary. The work of a bookkeeper will be useless unless consolidated and analyzed by an accountant. At the same time, an accountant cannot do any task unless he/she gets clear records from the bookkeeper. With that said, an accountant has a higher skill set and performs more complex tasks than a bookkeeper. For a person to qualify as an accountant, he/she must acquire a degree or CPA certification.

Since the bookkeeper provides the base documents or accounting, bookkeepers are required to know the basics of accounting too. Although it is not necessary for a bookkeeper to have formal training, the information they provide must be helpful to the accountant.

Duties of a Bookkeeper vs. an Accountant

The duties of a bookkeeper vary depending on the employer. There are some employers that will require bookkeepers to handle general financial management, including recording and organizing financial records and also offering accountancy services. In other cases, a bookkeeper will only be required to record financial transactions and forward them to the accountancy office. If you are starting out in business, you may maintain your books personally, instead of hiring a bookkeeper. Most startups do not hire bookkeepers or permanent accountants. If you can track down all the transactions yourself, just do simple bookkeeping and only bring in an accountant for payroll and tax processing or consultancy.

Some of the duties carried out by bookkeepers include:

1. Recommend, implement, or manage accounting software: In most cases, bookkeepers are in charge of recording, organizing, and managing of data. Therefore, they are better suited to recommend the best software, manage it, and implement it so that it offers value to the company.

2. Recommend, implement, and monitor bookkeeping

policies: The other duty of bookkeepers is to recommend policies that will make the process of bookkeeping smooth. At any level, a bookkeeper is required to reduce financial losses. The bookkeeper must look at loopholes and help employers deal with any discrepancies that may make the practice difficult.

3. Develop credit and debit accounts: The main duty of a bookkeeper is to maintain subsidiary books of accounts and the general ledger. For this duty, the bookkeeper must develop credit and debit accounts and assign expense categories.

4. Enter expenses and income into the software: It is the duty of the bookkeeper to ensure that all transactions are digitized. Since digital data is more reliable, modern bookkeepers will be required to digitize all documents, including checks and receipts.

5. Handle banking activities: In most companies, the bookkeeper is responsible for handling all banking activities. To ensure accountability and transparency, the bookkeeper is the center of cash flow. All the money coming and going outside the business must pass through the hands of the bookkeeper.

6. Train staff on the use of relevant bookkeeping software: If the company is using any bookkeeping software that requires all staff members to operate, the bookkeeper must train the other staff members on how to use the software.

7. Verify recorded transactions: It is the duty of a bookkeeper to consolidate the records and verify all the transactions. The bookkeeper has to look at the records and verify against documents such as receipts and checks that have been filled. If there are any discrepancies, the bookkeeper must correct them.

8. Verify the accuracy of the information and that the accounts balance.

9. Maintain records, and backup and archive, as necessary.

10. Assist the accountant in the preparation of financial statements: The bookkeeper may be required to help the accountant in preparing financial reports. In some companies, it is the bookkeeper that prepares financial reports. The first financial statement to be repaired is the trial balance and is always prepared by the bookkeeper.

11. Ensure bookkeeping adheres to accounting best practices and government regulations.

While the bookkeeper has so many duties, they are not as complex as those handled by the accountant. Some of the duties handled by accountants include:

1. Data Management: The accountant has the responsibility to oversee how data is recorded and stored. If the bookkeeper makes any mistakes in recording and storing financial transactions, it is the accountant who will suffer trying to prepare financial statements. To avoid such problems in the future, an accountant is required to ensure that all the data being recorded by the bookkeeper is recorded in the required formats and is credible.

2. Financial Analysis and Consultation: The other duty of the accountant is to offer advice on financial decisions. Once the financial statements are released, the accountant is better placed to interpret them and offer guidance on the best way forward for the company.

3. Financial Reports: The accountant is also responsible for generating financial reports required by the IRS and other bodies. Reports such as the balance sheet, the income sheet, etc., must be accurate and offer the true reflection of the company's performance. The accountant must ensure that any discrepancies that may occur along the way are handled and that the reports present the true figures of the company's

net worth and earnings.

4. Regulatory Compliance: Lastly, it is the duty of the accountant to ensure that the company is compliant with regulations. In this regard, accountants will be required to file taxes for employers and the company, process payroll, educate the board and employees on best financial practices and ensure that the company follows all the regulations put in place.

Key Accounting and Bookkeeping Principles

For any person practicing accounting, there are rules that must be followed. These rules are important in ensuring that there is transparency and a correlation between financial statements. If you are new to accounting, you must first understand these principles. As a matter of fact, understanding the accounting principles will make your work of learning to account much easier. The Generally Accepted Accounting Principles GAAPs are regulations that guide the practices of bookkeeping and accounting across the US and other parts of the world. These principles include.

Economic Entity Assumption

The first accounting principle is the assumption that every business is an economic entity. In other words, the business is operating with the aim of making a profit and growing in value. This assumption is vital in preparing financial statements. If we assume that an establishment is not interested in making a profit, there will be no need for preparing statements such as the profit and loss statement.

Monetary Unit Assumption

Another principle that guides accountancy states that all transactions must be recorded in the same currency. Although this principle does not dictate the currency to use, it requires that all transactions be recorded in one currency. For instance, you cannot record some transactions in British pounds then later change to US dollars. Even if a business operates offshore branches, the final financial reports must be presented in the same currency.

Specific Time Period Assumption

The other principle that guides accounting requires that all financial reports show results over a distinct period. Financial reports are not prepared in a vacuum. Every financial report must specify the period that is being reported. Some financial reports are prepared monthly, others quarterly, semi-annually, or annually. A business chooses the frequency of reporting in a year, in a bid to monitor its performances.

Cost Principle

The other principle that governs accounting is the cost principle. It states that the cost of an item does not change in financial reporting, the time of reporting withstanding. In other words, if an item is purchased today at $100, it must be reported that it is $100 even if the financial report is prepared 4 months later when the cost of the same item has doubled. Every transaction is recorded as it is at the time of the first operation and should not change even if the cost of the item in question changes.

Full Disclosure Principle

The principle requires that all information that relates to the function of a company's financial statements must be disclosed in notes accompanying statements. In other words, do not just provide financial statements without providing explanatory notes for items or figures that may not be understandable to all interested parties.

Going Concern Principle

This principle requires that a business' accounting be managed as if a business is a continuous entity that does not have an end in the near future. All businesses are assumed to have an infinite life and must be treated as such in accounting. Every counting period should give room for the transactions to occur in the following accounting periods.

Matching Principle

This principle requires that all businesses should use the accrual method of accounting and report financial information using this method. There are two methods of bookkeeping; the accrual and the cash method. In the cash method, transactions are recorded once money changes hands, while in the accrual method, transactions can be recorded before money changes hands. For instance, if you buy goods on credit, you can record this as a complete transaction under the accrual method. However, the cash method will only recognize this method after you have paid for the good.

Revenue Recognition Principle

The other principle of accounting is that revenue should be

reported when it is earned and not when it is received. This principle builds upon the accrual basis of bookkeeping. In this method, all transactions are deemed complete once they happen, regardless of whether money has been received or not. This principle mainly applies to limited companies and corporations. Smaller businesses such as sole proprietorships and partnerships may be exempted from some of the principles. A business that has revenue of less than $1,000,000 will not be subjected to most of these regulations.

Materiality Principle

The principle of materiality requires that accountants use their best judgment in case of an error. This principle recognizes the possibility of errors occurring in business transaction records. If the error is not significant, the accountants are required to take care of it by using their best judgment. In most cases, the accountants are expected to deal with the error in favor of the company as an entity they represent. However, errors that may have far-reaching effects cannot be corrected by assumptions. If the errors are too many, actions have to be taken to correct some.

Conservatism Principle

This principle states that, if there is more than one way of recording a transaction, liabilities and expenses should be recorded first and gains and revenues recorded later. This principle aims at protecting businesses from excess taxation due to poor record-keeping. Every time revenue and gains are recorded, the business taxes grow. However, liabilities and expenses reduce the taxes that are likely to be paid. This principle ensures that businesses do not suffer losses due to delayed entries that may end up being forgotten. If the gains are recorded first, the expenses may be forgotten, which might mean that a business will end up paying too much taxes.

Understanding these accounting principles will make your job easier and will help you learn accounting much faster. Take some time to review them and make sure you understand them well before we move on to the next chapter.

Chapter 2: Introduction to Financial Statements

Now that you know what accounting entails and the key principles that are used in accounting, let us have a look at financial statements. The whole of this book is based on preparing and interpreting financial statements. In this chapter, I am going to introduce you to financial statements, elaborate on their use, and help you know their importance in your business.

What are Financial Statements?

Financial statements are simply written records that are used to convey the activities of a business and the financial performance of the company. Financial statements are summarized information that is easy to interpret. The summary is made from data stored by bookkeepers. When a business operates on a day to day basis, the bookkeeper is required to keep records of all the transactions of the business. Over time, these transactions build-up and must be summarized to provide a clear view of the performance of the business. The information is summarized in key documents that are easy to interpret and follow the accounting principles mentioned above.

Financial statements must adhere to accounting best practices because they are legal documents. In other words, if the statements do not follow the set accounting principles, they may not be admissible in court in case of a legal battle. Further, financial statements are usually audited by responsible government agencies, accountants, other companies, etc. In other words, these summarized documents are important to many stakeholders. If you are running a business, your financial records will determine the amount of taxes you pay, the type of business partners you bring on board, and your credit worth, among other factors. It is, therefore, important for every business to prepare, organize, and file financial statements properly. The work of preparing, filing, and organizing records starts with proper bookkeeping, as already mentioned.

There are three main financial statements; the balance sheet, the income statement, and the cash flow statement. For any person who is new to the world of accounting, the focus should be on interpreting these key financial statements. However, there are other auxiliary financial statements that you may also want to prepare and interpret. You may be interested in the statement of owner's equity and statement of retained earnings, among others. In this book, we will mainly look at preparing and interpreting the balance sheet, the income statement, the cash flow statement, and the statement of owner's equity. These are the key financial statements that determine the future of any business. However, we will also look at the other financial statements and tools as we move on to help you have a clear understanding of your books.

The reason for picking out the four main financial records is that they can tell you everything you need to know about your business. The balance sheet provides an overview of the assets and liabilities of the company. From this overview, we are able to determine the position of the company in terms of financial stability. The income statement, on the other hand, focuses on the revenues and expenses of a company. As you can see, these two financial statements already cover everything you need to know about your business. The balance sheet helps you gauge the net worth of your business while the income statement helps you gauge the current performance of the business in terms of profits. The income statement will help you determine the net income of the business after deducting key expenses and taxes.

We will then look at the cash flow statement, which will help us measure how the company generates funds to pay its debts. The cash flow statement mainly focuses on operational costs and expenses. This statement tries to gauge the financial position of the company and the ability of the business to continue operating in the short term

Using Financial Statement Information

The information provided in financial statements is important to many people. Investors, financial analysts, tax authorities, and shareholders rely on the information provided in financial records in making decisions. For publicly traded businesses, the financial statements are very vital in providing guidance about the performance of such companies in the stock exchange market.

As you can see, we have different types of financial

statements. Each of the mentioned financial statements has its purposes and benefits.

Balance Sheets

The balance sheet is one of the most important financial statements for a business. It provides an overview of a company's assets, liabilities, and owner's equity. The balance sheet provides a picture of a company's net worth at a snapshot of time. This means that the assets and liabilities of the company are identified on the date when the balance sheet is prepared. Consequently, balance sheets have to keep on being prepared after some months to evaluate the growth of the company.

The balance sheet equation states that

$$Assets = Liabilities + Owner's\ equity$$

As you can see, the assets are added together to equal the sum of liabilities and owner's equity.

When we prepare the balance sheet, the aim is to recognize the growth of the business and determine its net worth. Assets are grouped on one side, and liabilities are grouped together with the owner's equity.

The balance sheet is a financial statement that can be prepared even before you start operating your business. As soon as you are ready to get started, prepare your first balance sheet so that it can help you gauge the net worth of your business in the future. From the equation, it is clear that a business's worth is its assets. However, the business's assets are either acquired from cash invested by the owner or cash borrowed. In other words, the cash invested by the owner at the start of the business represents the owner's equity, and cash borrowed represents liabilities. This is how simple a balance sheet can be at the start of a business. However, as the business starts operating and gaining profits or making losses, liabilities can grow or decrease; consequently, owners' equity can change, and assets will also change.

The main items included on a balance sheet in terms of assets include cash accounts, accounts receivable, and inventory. The liabilities to include to your balance sheet entail debts- both short term and long term, accounts payable, and dividends payable. The owner's equity is calculated separately after the income statement has been prepared, and all expenses paid.

Income Statements

While the balance sheet is prepared in a snapshot of time, the income statement is prepared over a period of time. The balance sheet is prepared on a specific date, and the items on the balance sheet represent the value of the company at that particular time. However, the income statement shows figures obtained over a specific trading period. The trading period in question may be 1 month, several months, or a year. Most businesses prepare their income statements quarterly, semi-annually, or annually. If you are running a small business, I will recommend preparing your financial statements in close succession to avoid prolonging mistakes. You could either prepare statements quarterly or semi-annually just to keep track of the performance of the business.

The formula for the income statement states that

Net Income = (Revenue–Expenses)

The main aim of the income statement is to determine the total revenue, expenses, and net profit of the business. If you choose to prepare your income statement after 3 months, it will show you the amount of money spent, generated, and the profit that the business has made over that period. The information needed to prepare the income statement is obtained from the general ledger. It is the general ledger that will record all your transactions (Expenses and revenues), which are needed to determine the net income of the profit. However, you must ensure that the information in the general ledger is accurate to help you prepare an accurate income statement. To test the accuracy of the general ledger, a trial balance is prepared.

Classifying Revenue and Expenses

When preparing the income sheet, you must first classify your revenue and expenses. Some businesses only have one source of revenue, which makes the entire process easy. If you are selling cars and do not have other sources of revenue, the process of preparing your income statement will be straight forward. The primary source of revenue for a business is the Operating Revenue (OR). This refers to the revenue obtained from the main business activity, such as selling cars in the example above. We also have other sources of revenue, such as interest earned on cash in the bank, rental income on a property, income from advertisement, and display, among others. Revenues can also be collected from the sale of long term assets such as land or vehicles. All these types of revenue are accounted for in the income statement.

Expenses can also be classified into primary and secondary expenses. Primary expenses include those that directly lead to the revenue generated. The primary expenses include the cost of goods sold and operational costs. The secondary expenses may include general administrative expenses, depreciation, research and development costs, among others.

The Cash Flow Statement

The third important income statement is the cash flow statement. This document offers a summary of the cash that flows into the business and out. The statement summarizes the debt of the business, its expenses, revenue, and fund investments. The document is mainly prepared as a complementary addition to the income statement and the balance sheet.

The information provided in the cash flow statement is mainly used by investors, especially potential partners. It provides information on whether the business is in a position to pay its debts and continue operating. There is no formula for the cash flow statement, but it is distributed into three sections: operating activities, financing activities, and investing activities.

The operating activities of the cash flow statement determine any sources of cash or uses of cash that occur due to running the business and selling goods and services. The operating CFS may include changes made in accounts receivable and payable, depreciation, and inventory. You should also include wages, taxes, and rent on this list.

Investing Activities

Investing activities, on the other hand, include any uses and gains of cash from long term investments. For instance, if the company made a loan to another company, and interest is being paid, such cash will be recorded under the investment activities. At the same time, if you have to pay interest on loans you acquired earlier, the amount will also be classified under investing activities.

Financing Activities

The financing activities include the sources of cash from investors, such as other companies or from banks. This section mainly deals with cash injection into the business other than what the business owns or dividends paid to shareholders. You may also include items such as stock purchases, equity issuance repayment debt, among others.

Statement of Owner's Equity

Finally, we have the statement of owner's equity. This is a financial statement that shows the portion of the company that belongs to the owners of the company. As we have already seen, the portion of the company owned by the founder of business on the day of starting is the capital invested. However, as days go by, the business may make profits and retain some of the profits in the business (Retained Earnings), which will increase the stake of the owner (Owners' Equity). The owner's equity is, therefore, calculated by adding retained earnings to the previous owner's equity.

Owner's Equity = Owner's Equity Brought Forward + Retained Earnings

The statement of owner's equity mainly shows the increase or decrease in the owner's capital at the start of the trading period. This means that the capital plus retained earnings at the end of the period is what we call the owner's equity. When preparing a statement of owner's equity, you will start with a heading, which will show the name of the company, the title of the report, and the period covered. If you are a sole proprietor, the title of your report should read "The Statement of owner's equity." If you are operating a partnership, the title should read "The statement of Partner's Equity." In corporations and public limited companies, we use the terms "The Statement of Stockholders' Equity."

Just like the income statement, the owner's equity is prepared at the end of a certain trading period. After preparing your income statement and determining your net income, you can proceed to distribute the income accordingly. Once all the income is distributed, and a portion is retained to be invested back to the company, add it to the owner's equity brought forward from the previous trading period.

The statement of owner's equity mainly depends on what happens in the income statement. Since we have established that the owner's equity is equal to the capital invested by owners of the business at the start, expenses will decrease the capital. At the same time, revenues will increase the capital. Given that the income statement aims at providing a net income figure, you can see that if the expenses are more than revenue, the income is likely to be negative. This will mean that capital will reduce, consequently leading to a reduction in owner's equity.

Why Financial Statements are Important

Financial statements are very crucial to businesses. Although each of the financial statements has its uses, let us look at the overall benefits of preparing financial statements for your business.

1. Track Financial position of the company: The balance sheet is a document that shows the position of the company financially. Without the balance sheet, it would be impossible for the company owners and other parties to know its net worth, its liabilities, and, as a result, the future of the business.

2. Evaluate the performance of a business: The other importance of income statements is that they help evaluate the past performance of the company. The income statement is particularly important in conveying information about the revenue and expenses of a company. Through this document, any interested party can determine the profits of the company and the sustainability of the business model. This information is important to investors, lenders, and government agencies. If you do not have credible financial statements to show the performance of your business, you may not be able to get funding even if you apply.

3. Show the current financial position of the company: The statement of cash flow is particularly important in displaying the current position of the company. When investors such as suppliers want to partner with your business, they must be assured that the company is in a position to pay its debts. The statement of cash flow helps show the strength of a business and its ability to finance debts. This is important to you as a business owner if you wish to secure trading partners too. If you do not provide accurate statements about your business's performance, chances are that your business will not be in good terms with lenders.

4. Shows net worth of the company: The other benefit of preparing financial statements is that you can determine the net worth of the company. From the balance sheet, we can have a look at the assets, liabilities, and owner's equity. The company's worth will only grow if the business is making profits and retaining them. All these factors will only be determined by looking at the various financial statements, including the balance sheet and the statement of owner's equity.

5. Planning for the future: The other importance of the financial statements is that they provide information that will help the management plan for the future. As the business owner or manager, you should think about future

investments and make informed decisions to help the company grow. Without having a clear understanding of the current company's financial position, you cannot make such key decisions. The income statement helps the management by providing information that makes the work of decision making easier.

6. Guide shareholders in making investments: The income statement can also be used by shareholders to make key decisions. If you are a shareholder, you want to invest in a business that is making profits and is showing prospects of growth for the future. This information can only be obtained by looking at the financial statements. The income statement and the balance sheet will help you know if the company is on an upward growth trend or on a downward spiral. These statements are very vital for both current and prospective investors. Even though an individual might not have any shares in the company, the information provided may help any prospective investors make the best decisions.

7. Guide for creditors and lenders: Besides prospective investors and shareholders, lenders and creditors also need to look at financial statements. The income statement and the statement of cash flow are very vital for creditors and debtors. They determine the financial liquidity of a company, the debt ratio, profitability, and the return on investment of

the company. All these indicators will determine how the business operates in the future.

If a business has more current debts than current assets, it means that it lacks operating capital. In other words, it might not be able to meet its short term liabilities. For such a business, creditors and lenders may not want to engage in business. It is therefore vital that all this information is made available by providing accurate financial statements.

8. Employees Compensation: The income statements also provide guidance on employee compensation. When we look at the financial statements, we can tell that a business is operating in profit or loss. The employees of a company use such information to review their wages and possibilities of a future appraisal. If you are working for a company that keeps on making losses year in year out, chances are that you should be looking for another job. Such information by companies helps employees plan for their future with the current employer.

9. Calculating taxes to be paid: Without financial statements, it is not possible to determine the amount of tax a company is supposed to pay. For this reason, all businesses are required to prepare financial records. The government uses the provided financial records to arrive at the decision of

how much tax business will pay. As a company, you may also be overtaxed if you do not provide accurate financial information. In this regard, it is important to prepare the most accurate financial statements for your business.

10. Debt management: The information available in financial statements is also very important to the management of the company. If you are the manager, you need to know the company's debt level, liquidity, cash flow, among other factors. The information provided in financial statements will help you start managing your debts properly, control lending and borrowing.

11. Trend Analysis: For every business, it is important to look at the trends and try to invest based on the performance of the business. Without financial reports, it would be difficult to determine the trend of the business. For instance, the profit and loss statement provides figures about sales and expenditure. Through such statements, you can determine areas of expenditure that are hurting the company and the products that bring in the most revenue. This Way, you can make informed marketing and production decisions that will foster the growth of your business.

12. Tracking: The management of the business also enjoys a clear view of the future. Financial tracking will help

eliminate possible roadblocks before they happen. You can detect the possibility of supply chain problems just by looking at your cash flow reports and making decisions that will facilitate smooth operations of the business in the future.

13. Compliance: Last but not least, every business must be able to comply with government authorities in many areas. The main area of concern when it comes to business finances is the payment of taxes and employee wages. Without financial statements, it is not possible to detect the amount of tax a company is required to pay.

For this reason, it is a government requirement that all businesses prepare accurate financial statements and make the public. Every company is required to audit its finances, verify the information, and make it readily available for government audits. This helps to ensure that there is transparency.

Who Needs to See Financial Statements?

We have already looked at some of the parties who may be interested in your financial statements. However, the list of interested parties is longer than you may imagine. Some of the parties interested in seeing your financial statements may not have good intentions, but you are required to make your information freely available. The parties that will need the financial statements include:

1. Company management: The management team of the company is the first beneficiary of financial statements. They need the information to determine the liquidity of the company, profitability, and determine cash flows. This information is necessary to help maintain day to day operations of the company.

2. Competitors: Competitors and brands that are similar to yours will try to gain insight into your financial information. The information obtained from financial reports can be used in a competitive market structure. For instance, if your competitor notices that you are gaining a lot of revenue from a certain line of products, they may choose to invest in the same line and compete for your market share.

3. Customers: When most people prepare financial statements, they don't consider the implications they may have on customers. However, customers are among the parties that need financial statements. Most customers review financial statements before awarding tenders to suppliers. From the financial statements, the customer can tell the company that will meet the quality and quantity of

goods needed.

4. Employees: As we have already seen, employees also need to monitor the financial position of a company. If the company keeps on making losses, an employee may choose to take off before they are left jobless. From the financial reports, employees can also find a reason to bargain for better terms.

5. Governments: Government agencies also need to review financial reports for the purposes of taxation. Any company that makes profits is required to pay taxes to government agencies in the regions where it is located. For this reason, governments will be required to look at the financial documents of your business.

6. Investment analysts: If you happen to hire an investment analyst for your business, he/she cannot offer any analysis unless you provide the right data. The information needed to make key investment decisions is only available in financial statements. For this reason, you must ensure that you prepare accurate financial statements for your business.

7. Investors: Investors who wish to partner with your business or inject capital must also look at financial statements. As already mentioned, you will not be able to

secure lending for your business unless you have the proper financial statements. Be it banks, individuals, or other credit facilities, the main point of reference when investing in a business is the financial statements.

8. Rating agencies: All businesses undergo ratings at some point. The ratings determine the success of a business in terms of its creditworthiness. If a credit rating company deems your company unworthy of receiving credit, you will not survive for long. Such agencies depend on the financial data provided to calculate your credit. They base your credit on the available resources such as assets, capital, and owner's equity.

9. Suppliers: The other group of people who will benefit and must look at your financial statement is that of suppliers. Suppliers mainly use financial statements to determine whether a client is the right fit for a business corporation.

10. Unions: Lastly, unions also use the information provided in financial statements. They must be sure that a company is in a position to pay union fees to retain its membership. Employee unions also look at accompanying books when lobbying for employee rights. They must prove that a company is making sufficient money before demanding a pay rise and other perks.

Chapter 3: Preparation and Interpreting Financial Statements

Now, we have the section where we prepare and analyze all the above-mentioned financial statements. Since I promised to make your work as simple as possible, we may use shortcuts and simple examples to make everyone understand how each of the important financial statements is prepared. From the chapters above, we have already established that the main financial statements entail the balance sheet, the income statement, and the cash flow statement. However, for the sake of making the process of accounting much easier, we will include other documents in this chapter, such as the trial balance and the statement of owner's equity.

Preparing and Interpreting the Trial Balance

Although the trial balance is not classified as a major financial statement, it is the basis for preparing all the financial statements. Essentially, the general ledger is the basis for preparing all the other financial statements. However, a general ledger might have errors. Preparing the trial balance will help us deal with any errors that may have occurred in the general ledger.

The main reason I have included the trial balance on this list is to help you see how financial statements are developed from one piece of information to another. My assumption is that you already have a bookkeeper and a well-organized ledger book. The entire process of accounting starts with a bookkeeper recording all transactions in specialty accounts. Once the transactions accumulate, they are summarized and recorded in the general ledger.

The general ledger transactions are then summarized under specific accounts at the close of the trading period. It is at this point where we have to prepare a trial balance to verify whether the information recorded in the general ledger is up to date. If the information is not accurate, we may never be able to prepare an accurate income statement, which will mean that we won't arrive at the right statement of owner's equity and, consequently, an erroneous balance sheet.

In the simplest terms possible, the trial balance lists the closing balances of credit and debit transactions over a given trading period.

For instance, if your business has been operating from January to December, the trial balance tries to compare the transactions over this period to see whether they balance. The equation for the trial balance states that

$$Assets + Expenses + Drawings = Liabilities + Revenue + Owners\ Equity$$

This equation shows that the assets of a business summed up with expenses and withdrawals from the business must add up to the liabilities, revenue, and owner's equity. In other words, all the assets and expenses of the business can only be funded by money borrowed (liability), money earned (revenue), or money invested (owners' equity/ capital).

Trial Balance for year ended XXX

Particulars	Debit	Credit
	Balance	
Bank	28,000	
Cash	12,000	
Debtors	43,000	
Provision for doubtful debts		2,000
Fixed assets	1,30,000	
Accumulated depreciation		14,000
Mutual fund investments	35,000	
Prepaid expenses	8,000	
Share capital		1,20,000
Reserves and surplus		50,000
Bank loan		32,000
Interest payable		8,000
Creditors		10,000
Sales		90,000
Purchases	50,000	
Depreciation expense	4,000	
Rent expense	3,000	
Other expenses	13,000	
	3,26,000	**3,26,000**

As you can see from the sample trial balance above, all the credit entries sum up with all the debit entries; hence the equation works.

The first step to preparing a trial balance is to consolidate all the balances in the ledger accounts and cash book.

Once you have all the information you need, prepare a 3 column worksheet. The first column should hold the account name, the second column debit, and the third column credit balances.

Now fill out the account name and the corresponding balances in the appropriate debit or credit column.

In the end, total the credit balances and the debit balances. They should be equal.

For simplicity, arrange the balances of the following accounts on the debit side of your trial balance:

Assets

Expense Accounts

Drawings Account

Cash Balance

Bank Balance

Any losses

For the credit side of the trial balance, arrange the following accounts balances:

Liabilities

Income Accounts

Capital Account

Profits

If the trial balance does not balance well, chances are that there are some mistakes in your data. Some of the mistakes that may lead to failure of the trial balance from balancing include:

An error made when transferring the information from the general ledger to your trial balance.

An error in adding up the sum of the amounts on either side of the trial balance.

An error in recording the amounts in the general ledger.

Making an entry in the wrong column. I.e., making a credit entry in the debit column.

A mistake made in the general ledger or subsidiary books of entry.

Benefits of the Trial Balance

The trial balance offers plenty of benefits to the business owner. This document is mostly used internally and is rarely required by external parties. Some of the benefits of the document include:

1. To verify that debits are equal to credits: If the debits and credits are not equal, there are chances that there are some errors in the accounting or bookkeeping process. It is the work of the accountant and bookkeeper to find such errors and correct them.

2. To find the uncovered errors in journalizing: This document will help you detect any errors occurring in subsidiary books of entry. If you cannot balance the accounts, errors must be tracked back to the root.

3. To find the uncovered errors in posting: The trial balance also helps the accountant detect errors occurring due to wrong entries or posting.

4. To make financial statements: The trial balance is the

primary document that lays the ground for preparing the other financial statements. It is not recognized as a financial statement, but it must be present for you to prepare the other financial statements.

5. To list the accounts at a single place: The trial balance helps reconcile all the accounts in one place. In most cases, accounts are recorded in specialty books, which can be hard to track.

Shortcomings of the Trial Balance

With all the benefits offered by the trial balance, the statement also has a lot of shortcomings. This document is vital for the internal correction of errors, but it may not be helpful in some instances due to the following shortcomings.

1. The trial balance cannot prove that all transactions have been recorded. For instance, if you omit a transaction on both credit and debit sides, the trial balance will still balance, even though a crucial transaction is missing.

2. It does not prove whether the ledger entries are wrong or correct. For instance, if you make an entry error such that, instead of recording $400, you enter $4000, the trial balance will balance well as long as the figure is recorded on

both sides.

3. It cannot find any missing entries from the journal.

Preparing and Interpreting the Income Statement

The income statement or the profit and loss statement is a summary of the income and expenditure of a business over a trading period. As we have already seen, the income statement summarizes the financial performance of a business over a given period of time. We have already established that the data needed to prepare the income statement is obtained from the general ledger. From your recorded transactions, determine the expenses and the revenues and compile them in a table to determine your net incomes. Here is a step by step guide on how to prepare the income statement.

Step 1: Calculate the Gross Profit

The first step in preparing the income statement is determining the gross profit. When preparing the income statement, the items are systematically arranged on a template. The first item at the top of your list is the total revenue. As we have already seen, you can calculate the total revenue by adding revenue from the sale of goods and services with revenues from other sources such as interests or sales of assets. Once you have the total revenue subtract direct costs from it to determine the gross profit.

Gross Profit = Gross Revenue- Direct Costs

The gross profit is the income made by the company before deducting indirect expenses such as operational costs, taxes, etc. You can express the gross profit in percentage, which is known as the gross margin.

Gross Margin = Gross profit/Gross Revenue

For example, if you sell t-shirts in an uptown shop and you purchase 100 t-shirts at the cost of $10 each. Your direct expenses would be $1000. If you were to sell all the t-shirts at the price of $12 each, your total income would be $120. Your gross profit, in this case, would be $120- $100=$20, and the gross margin would be ($20/$120) x 100 =16.6%

The gross margin indicates the financial stability of the business. If your business has a higher gross margin, it is performing well and is likely to remain afloat for a longer period. However, a low gross margin might mean that you need to change some aspects of your operations to reduce expenses or increase revenue.

Step 2: Calculate Earnings Before Interest and Taxes (EBIT)

On your income sheet template, you are also going to calculate the earnings before interest and taxes. This value represents the income the company would have made if it were not required to pay taxes or interest on loans. This value is arrived at by deducting the cost of goods and operational expenses from the gross revenue. Since we have already subtracted the cost of goods from the gross revenue to determine the gross profit, the simplest way to determine EBIT is by subtracting operational expenses from your gross profit. Operational costs are the normal daily expenses of a business, such as rent, electricity, etc.

EBIT= Gross Profit - Operational Costs

Step 3: Calculate the Earnings Before Tax (EBT)

Once you have obtained your EBIT value, you should determine the earnings of the company before tax. Most small business owners make the mistake of assuming that the EBIT is the true income of business before tax. In reality, the true earning of business before tax must account for depreciation. Through day to day operations, a business is likely to lose some value from its assets. You must, therefore, calculate the value of depreciation and subtract from the EBIT value to determine the earnings before tax.

EBT= EBIT- Depreciation

Step 4: Calculate the Net Income

Lastly, calculate the net income of the business to determine whether the company makes a profit or loss during the trading period in question. The EBT value above does not show the true earnings of your business. To determine the net income, you have to subtract indirect expenses from the earnings before taxes. Some of the indirect expenses include taxes and insurance costs.

Net profit/loss =EBT- Indirect expenses

The main purpose of preparing the income sheet is to determine whether the business is making profits or losses. The formula above gives a final value of your income, and that will be your net income or loss. It is important to note that the value you get will depend on your accuracy. If you fail to include some expenses or revenues in your income sheet, you are likely to get a false value. Businesses operate based on different models. In other words, you should try to understand your business model and use your best judgment to ensure that all the sources of revenue and expenses are accounted for in the income sheet.

If you are new to accounting, you may find using an accounting software complex. For those who do not know how to use complex accounting tools, just stick to using the basic MS excel. Microsoft's excel provides easy to use income sheet templates that you can use to prepare your income sheet.

Here is an example of a simple income sheet.

Income Statement
For Year Ending December 31, 2012

Sales		$50,00,000
Cost of Goods Sold		
Materials	8,00,000	
Labor	11,00,000	
Overhead	6,00,000	25,00,000
Gross Margin		**$25,00,000**
Operating Expenses		
Selling Expenses	9,00,000	
Administrative Expenses	6,00,000	
Depreciation and Amortization	5,00,000	2000000
Operating Income		**$5,00,000**
Other Income & Expenses		
Interest Revenue	50000	
Interest Expense	-1,00,000	
Extraordinary items	2,00,000	1,50,000
Income Before Tax		$6,50,000
Income Tax (at 35%)		$2,27,500
Net Income		**$4,22,500**

Preparing and Interpreting the Balance Sheet

The balance sheet is a statement that shows the book value of a business. As we have already mentioned, you can even prepare a balance sheet on the first day of your business. However, once your business starts operating, the value of your business starts changing due to profit and losses being made from daily operations. For this reason, it is necessary to prepare the income statement before you think about preparing the balance sheet.

As we have already seen, the balance sheet is made up of 3 key items; the assets, liabilities, and owners' equity. The reason why I recommend preparing the income sheet before preparing the balance sheet is that you must first calculate your owner's equity to be able to balance your balance sheet.

The balance sheet is very important to the owners of the business as well as the external users. For the owner of the business, the balance sheet makes it possible to determine the assets of the company. It is through reviewing the assets of the company that the owners can plan for the future. The balance sheet also provides a vivid picture of the liabilities and the value of the company as a whole. As we have seen, the formula for the balance sheet states that.

Assets = Liabilities + Shareholders' Equity

Step1: Determine the Reporting Date and Period

The first step when it comes to preparing the balance sheet is determining the reporting date. As we have mentioned, a balance sheet is prepared at a snapshot of time. In other words, it is used to show the value of a company on a specific date. When preparing the balance sheet, you need to account for assets, liabilities, and owner's equity on the date of preparation. The date you choose is usually referred to as the reporting date. For most businesses, a balance sheet can be prepared quarterly, semi-annually, or annually. For those who prepare quarterly, they have to prepare 4 balance sheets in a year. This type of reporting provides the best platform for reviewing the growth of the business. The quarterly approach is used to review the growth of the business closely, especially for those who run small businesses.

Companies that use the annual approach usually review their books on 31st December. However, you may choose a date that you find ideal for your business. On the specific date, compile your business's assets, liabilities, and owner's equity to determine the value of your business.

Step 2: Identify Your Assets

Once you have selected your reporting date, start by reviewing all your assets on the date of balance sheet preparation. Usually, we list each asset in its line then sum up the assets, as you can see from the balance sheet below. We have provided entries for cash, stock, accounts receivable, etc. All these components are assets and must be listed individually.

The value for most of the assets can be obtained from your ledger book. At the start of every trading period, all balances from the previous trading period are brought forward into the new trading period ledger book.

This means that your general ledger should contain all the information you need to prepare your balance sheet.

To simplify your work when preparing the balance sheet, list your item as current assets and long-term assets.

The items to include among the current assets are cash and cash equivalents, accounts receivable, marketable securities, inventory, and other current assets.

Under the long term assets section, you may list items such

as company property, long term market securities, goodwill, etc.

When we prepare a balance sheet, we use a template that is divided into two main sections. One section will total the assets, and the other section will total the liabilities and owner's equity. If you don't know how to format the template for a balance sheet, just use the MS Excel balance sheet template shown below.

BALANCE SHEET

DATE

ASSETS

	2012	2013
Current Assets		
Cash	1,200	1,400
Temporary Investments		
Inventories		
Accounts receivable		
Prepaid expenses		
Other		
Total Current Assets	1,200	1,400
Fixed Assets		
Property, land and equipment		
Leasehold improvements		
Equity and other long-term investments		
Intangible assets		
Less accumulated depreciation (Negative Value)	- 300	- 195
Total Assets	- 300	- 195
Other Assets		
Deferred income tax		
Charity/Goodwill		
Other		
Total Other Assets	-	-
TOTAL ASSETS	900	1,205

LIABILITIES AND OWNER'S EQUITY

	2012	2013
Current Liabilities		
Accounts payable		350
Accrued wages and salaries		
Accrued compensation	600	
Short-term loans		
Income taxes payable		
Unearned revenue	300	
Current portion of long-term debt		
Total Current Liabilities	900	350

Step 3. Identify Your Liabilities

Once you are done with identifying and listing your assets, it is time to identify and list all your liabilities. Just like we did with assets, you should list your liabilities as current and long term. The items to include among current liabilities are accrued expenses, accounts payable, deferred revenue, the current value of long-term loans, etc. Under the long term liabilities section, you can include items such as deferred revenue, long term lease obligations, long term liabilities, among others. Include the subtotal for current liabilities and long term liabilities, then provide the final figure on the total liabilities.

Step 4: Calculate Shareholders' Equity

Once you are done with listing and calculating the value for current and long term assets and liabilities, you need to calculate the owner's equity. If you are running a sole proprietorship, calculating the owner's equity is simple and direct. However, for a publicly-traded company, a lot of factors have to be considered when calculating the owner's equity. Some of the items to include to your shareholder's equity section are common stock, preferred stock, treasury stock, and retained earnings.

If you have the balance sheet prepared for the previous reporting date, you can use it to calculate the owner's equity easily. In a sole proprietorship, the owner's equity can simply be calculated by adding retained earnings to the previous owner's equity.

> Owners' equity = Owners equity from previous period + Retained earnings

This means that, before you prepare your balance sheet, you must first determine the value of retained earnings. I will show you later how to calculate retained earnings when we look at preparing the statement of owner's equity.

Step 5: Compare the sum of Assets with that of Liabilities and Owner's Equity

Once you have arrived at the value of the owner's equity, you should compare the sums of assets to that of liabilities and owner's equity. If the value of the two does not balance, chances are that there are errors in your calculations. You may either have used the wrong figures, or you may have imported the wrong figures from the general ledger.

Balance sheet for XYZ business on the 31st of December 2010		
	$	$
ASSETS		
Non-current assets		2,150,000
Land and buildings	2,000,000	
Furniture	12,000	
Machinery	18,000	
Investments	120,000	
Current assets		10,000
Inventory	1,000	
Debtors / receivables	3,200	
Bank and cash	5,800	
TOTAL ASSETS		2,160,000
EQUITY AND LIABILITIES		
Owner's equity		1,700,000
Capital	1,700,000	
Non-current liabilities		440,000
10% Loan	440,000	
Current liabilities		20,000
Creditors / payables	20,000	
TOTAL EQUITY AND LIABILITIES		2,160,000

As you can see from the balance sheet above, the section for assets is summed up differently. The sum of the assets equals the sum of liabilities and the owner's equity.

Preparing and Interpreting the Statement of Cash Flows

The next most important financial statement is the statement of cash flows. The statement of cash flows helps us determine the ability of a business to continue running its day to day business operations. When preparing the statement of cash flows, we divide the template into three sections. This is because the statement of cash flows is divided into cash flows from investing activities, financing activities, and operation activities, as we have already seen in the chapters above.

1. Operating activities cash flow: This refers to the money that the business spends on running day to day operations. Some of the activities to include under the operating cash flows include the money obtained from the selling of goods and services, money spent on paying rent, salaries, etc. Negative cash flows are subtracted from the positive cash flows when preparing the statement of cash flows. For instance, the money used in paying salaries has to be subtracted from the money earned from selling goods and services.

2. Investing activities cash flow: This refers to the money earned or spent from market securities or long term assets. For instance, money earned from selling and buying of fixed assets and marketable securities, among others. In simple terms, the money spent or earned from other investment activities apart from day to day business operations fall under this category.

3. Financing activities cash flow: The other section of the cash flow statement will include money earned or spent on financing activities. This includes the amount of money earned or spent due to cash or cash related transactions between the company and its owners, investors, or lenders. For instance, if the owners of the business take dividends from the business, it will be listed under the financing activities. At the same time, owners injecting capital or borrowing money from lenders can also fall under investing activities.

Step 1: Gather Cash Flows from Operations

The first step involves gathering and listing all the cash flows from operations. Cash Flows from operations are easy to gather, given that all the information is already available in your profit and loss statement. Any information that you may lack in your profit and loss document should be available in your ledger books.

The first item to list on your cash flow from operations is the earnings before interest and Taxes EBIT. You will also have to calculate the value for depreciation and include it on your cash flow statement. To get a clear picture of your cash flows, you must calculate the value for depreciation so that you do not end up overestimating the financial capacity of your business. Once you have obtained the value of depreciation, calculate the cash flows from operating activities using the formula.

Cash flow from operating activities = EBIT + Depreciation

As you can see from the example provided below, some of the values are in brackets while others are not. In most cases, the value of cash flows can be either positive or negative. The positive values represent cash flow activities that bring money into the business. On the other hand, negative cash flows represent activities that take money outside the business. Normally, we place the negative values in brackets instead of using a negative sign. For instance, if your EBIT value is $4000 and the depreciation value is $500, we will still use the formula shown above when listing the items, but in reality, we will subtract depreciation from the EBIT value. This is how we will represent the items on our statement of cash flows.

EBIT $4000

Depreciation ($500)

Operating cash flows ($3500)

This shows that, although we add depreciation to EBIT value, we are supposed to subtract because the depreciation takes money from the business.

Step 2: Calculate Cash Flow from Investing Activities

Once you are done with calculating the cash flows from operating activities, follow the same process to calculate cash flows from investing activities. As we have already seen, investing activities are those that add money to the business for investments or money that is drawn out of the business to investments.

Activities that can be categorized under-investing include selling of long term assets, collecting settlement, loaning out money, collecting loans, etc.

Although we classify giving out loans and collecting loaned money under investing activities, loans received by your business from lenders are classified under financing activities. At the same time, money used on paying loans should also be classified under financing activities.

To calculate your investing activities cash flows, simply list the items in this section as we did with the operating activities above and subtract the negative cash flows from the positive cash flows.

Step 3: Calculate Cash Flow from Financing Activities

Lastly, calculate the cash flows from financing activities. In this section, just list the positive financing activities and list the negative ones. As we have seen, financing activities are those that add money to the business or remove money from the business to the business owners, creditors, or investors.

For instance, if an investor were to pump money into the business to facilitate its running, that amount can be classified as a financing activity. The items to include in your financing activities cash flows are long term loans and payment for such loans, capital injection by owners, and collection of dividends, among others.

Statement of Cash Flows
(For the year ended December 31, 2005)

Cash flows provided from operating activities		
Net Income		33,000
Depreciation Expense		10,000
Increase in Accounts Receivable	(26,000)	
Increase in Accounts Payable	7,000	(19,000)
Net cash provided by operating activities		24,000
Cash flows provided from investing activities		
Purchase of Building	(19,000)	
Sale of Long-Term Investment	35,000	
Net cash provided by investing activities		16,000
Cash flows provided from financing activities		
Payment of Dividends	(12,000)	
Issuance of Common Stock	10,000	
Net cash provided by financing activities		(2,000)
Net increase (decrease) in cash		38,000
Cash at the beginning of the year		165,000
Cash at the end of the year		203,000

Once you have prepared the various cash flows, compile them in a final summary document. You will have to add the cash flows from the operating activities to that from investing and financing activities. If any of the cash flows are negative, deduct it instead of adding. For instance, if you have more money going out in the investing activities section than the money coming in, the chances are that your cash flows from investing activities will be negative. If the final value of cash flows from investing activities is negative, you will have to deduct it from the sum of the other two sections to determine the final value. If the cash flows from all the three investing activities are negative, you will have to add them together and place the final value in brackets to indicate that they are negative.

Preparing and Interpreting the Statement of Owner's Equity

Finally, we have to prepare and interpret the statement of owner's equity. The statement of owner's equity is an important document that helps determine the value of the company that is owned by the owners of the business. However, before we calculate the owner's equity, we must first calculate retained earnings. Look at our balance sheet above, and you will see how the owner's equity is calculated.

In the simplest terms, retained earnings are a portion of the earnings that the company does not distribute to shareholders. It can be used to grow the business in the outlined ways. The value of retained earnings increases if the business makes a profit and reduces if a business makes a loss. Since stakeholders' equity is a key part of the balance sheet, retained income must be shown as a component of stakeholder's equity.

The statement of retained earnings is used to determine the

portion of a company's earnings that are retained in the business from the profit made. The retained earnings of a company are calculated by adding the retained earnings for the period in question to the retained earnings from the previous trading period. In other words, retained earnings of a company are compounded over a long period. If the company retained 30% of its profits during the first year of operation, the retained earnings for the second year of operations would be the value of the money that has to be retained from profits during that year plus the amount of retained earnings in the first year. This means that the value of retained earnings can grow or decrease depending on whether the company makes profits or losses in a given trading period. Retained earnings at the end of a trading period are calculated by the formula.

Retained Earnings = Beginning Balance of RE + Net (Profit/loss) - Dividends

As you can see from the formula, the amount of retained earnings brought forward must be used to arrive at the current retained earnings.

Once you get the value for retained earnings, use it to calculate the owner's equity. The owner's equity of any company is the portion of the company that can be claimed by the owners. Just like it is the case with retained earnings, owner's equity is compounded. To determine the owner's equity, you will have to determine the beginning balance of the owner's equity, then add investments by owners and retained earnings.

Owner's Equity = Beginning Balance + Investments by Owners ± Retained earnings

Chapter 4: What You Can Learn From Financial Statements

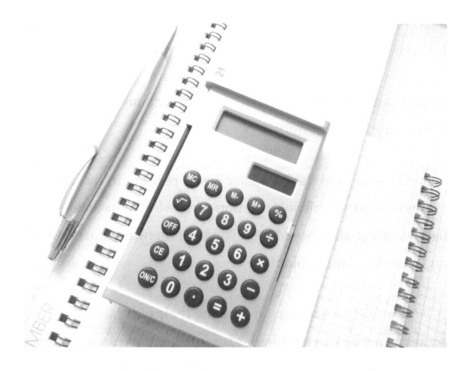

After preparing financial statements, you should be able to interpret them and understand what they mean. In case you are the manager or the owner of the business, you may not even be interested in preparing financial statements, but rather interpreting them. In this chapter, we are going to look at the interpretation of financial statements. We have to find out what each statement means, what the figures represent, and how you can use the information in your day to day business operations. At the end of the day, all the information provided in the financial statements should add value to your business. If you cannot interpret the various financial statements, you will have a hard time making key business decisions and even fail to achieve the growth targets for your business.

By learning to read and interpret your company's financial documents, you can find out:

1. The level of debt the company has in relation to the available equity. This information can be found in your balance sheet and should help you plan on future borrowings and debt repayment plans.

2. How quickly customers are paying their bills after products have been supplied. This information can be obtained from your income sheet and will help you manage your cash flows.

3. Whether there is a decline or increase in short term cash. This information can be obtained from the cash flow statement and is vital for a company to continue managing day to day operations.

4. The number of assets that are tangible and long term. This information can be obtained from the balance sheet and will help you plan for your long term investments.

5. Whether products are being returned or purchased at rates higher than in previous instances. This information can be obtained from the income statement and can be used to manage product production and marketing.

6. The number of days or months it takes for your business to sell its inventory. This information can be obtained from the income sheet and will help plan for future marketing and production.

7. Whether the money invested in infrastructure and development is giving any results and whether the results are viable for the future. You can determine this information from your cash flow and owner's equity statements and use it to plan your future investments.

8. Whether there is a decline in the interest coverage ratio on bonds. This information can be obtained from the balance sheet and owners' equity statements and can be used to plan for future investments.

9. The interest rates that the company pays on its debts. This

information can be determined from the cash flow statement and is important in deciding future financing activities. If the company spends too much money on repaying loans due to high-interest rates, you could restructure the loan repayment plans to reduce the burden the company to undergo.

10. Where the profits earned by the company are invested or spent. Such information can be found in your cash flow statements and can help plan for future investments.

The information available in these key documents must be applied to the day to day running of your business. Most people who manage or run businesses should be informed on the use of the financial information provided by financial statements. Although the accountant might be obligated to elaborate on all the information provided in the books of accounts, they may still lie about some of the information to mislead your decision making. It is, therefore, necessary to invest in the right tools to help you make informed decisions.

Learning from the Balance Sheet

The balance sheet is a very important statement that can help you learn a lot of information about your business. As we have already seen from the balance sheet equation.

$$Assets = Liabilities + Owner's\ equity$$

This means that you can get information about your assets, liabilities, and owner's equity. Just by comparing two balance sheets prepared in consecutive periods, you can tell whether your company assets are growing or declining. You can also determine the growth and decline in liabilities and owner's equity. For any business, the financial strength of the company is measured by the value of assets and owner's equity. If your business has more liabilities than assets and owner's equity, chances are that your business is very unstable financially.

While just looking at the balance sheet might give you an idea of where your business is heading, the naked eye does not provide detailed information. For all financial statements, we use financial ratios to analyze the information provided and determine the meaning of the information. For instance, you may realize that your company has more liabilities than assets and start thinking that it is headed downhill. In reality, some business models can support high debts as long as they remain operational. For this reason, we use analysis tools known as financial ratios to analyze the financial statements.

When analyzing the balance sheet, the main ratios used

include the debt to equity ratio and the working capital ratio.

1. The Debt to Equity Ratio: The debt to equity ratio is calculated by dividing the total companies liabilities by the total shareholder's equity. In other words, this formula can help determine the level of debt as compared to the owner's equity. If your stake in the company is less than your debts, it becomes a high risk since even if the business were to end at any time, the company might not be able to pay its debts accordingly. All the information you need to calculate the debt to equity ratio is available on your balance sheet.

Debt to equity ratio (D/E) = Total liabilities/Owners Equity.

Since the debt to equity ratio is used to measure a company's debts relative to the owner's equity, it is a good tool that can help you measure the value of net assets. In other words, the net assets of the company equal to the total assets less total long-term liabilities. If the company has a high debt to equity ratio, it shows that the company relies on debts to purchase its assets. If the company has a lower debt to equity ratio, it shows that a company does not rely on debts to finance its assets.

For different business models, the debt to equity ratio

allowed varies. In some businesses, a high debt to equity ratio is okay. If the high debt to equity ratio is helping the business grow and expand its operations in a healthy way, you do not have to worry. However, if the debt to equity ratio remains high, yet the business operations are not expanding, the business is likely to topple. At the end of the day, if you are borrowing to increase operations, make more money, and grow the business, you are on the right track.

A high debt to equity ratio is often considered high risk. However, since the debt to equity ratio offers the platform for business growth, most people often compare the owner's equity to long term debts to get a clearer picture of the company's operations. For instance, if your business relies on supplies that provide goods on credit, you may end up having a high debt to equity ratio that does not pose any risk to your business. On the other hand, if the debt to equity ratio is high, and you happen to have more long term liabilities, chances are that the business is at high risk.

2. Working Capital: The other important ratio that you must consider when analyzing your balance sheet is the working capital ratio. The working capital ratio is simply the difference between your current assets and current liabilities. This ratio does not consider the future of a business, but rather looks at the short term needs of a business. The

working capital determines whether a business can run its current operations well without the need for external funds. If your business has a high working capital ratio, it means that your business can run smoothly in the short run. You do not have to borrow heavily to finance your current needs. However, a business that relies on borrowed funds to run the day to day operations may get stuck at any moment.

3. Net Operating Capital: This is the other ratio that will help make your interpretation of the balance sheet easier. This ratio is the measure of a company's liquidity. It refers to the differences between current operating assets and current operating liabilities. These figures can be obtained from a company's receivable plus inventories.

If a company has a positive operating capital, it has the potential to grow. You can invest the capital available to expand your production and work towards having a larger share of the market. From your balance sheet, you should determine the amount of capital that is available at your disposal and whether it is enough to keep your business running. If the company has more liabilities than assets, you can inject more capital to improve the operating capital. At the end of the day, having more liabilities may also mean that your company is spending most of the earnings to pay debts.

All these financial strength ratios give you an indication of the strength of the company. They may help you determine how the company finances its activities and the financial stability of the company. Such ratios show the strength of the company and the ability to finance its cycle.

Through such ratios, you can find a lot of information about the balance sheet. The balance sheet can also be used to monitor the growth of the company over a long period. If you can review your assets and liabilities as compared to the start of your business, you will determine the rate of growth of the business over the years.

Learning from the Income Statement

Besides the balance sheet, you also have to interpret your income statement and use the figures provided accurately. When it comes to the income statement understanding the figures can be pretty straightforward, as long as your accountant breaks them into small chunks. However, if the accountant ends up lumping large chunks of numbers together, it becomes complex to understand your financial statements. For instance, in our procedure to prepare the income statement, we broke the income statement into 4 sections. We start by determining the gross profit and then calculate the gross margin. We then go further to determine the earnings before interest and tax then determine the earnings before tax. Finally, we determine the net income (earnings after tax and other expenses). In some instances, a balance sheet might be summarized in such a way that you only get the total revenue less total expenses. In such a case, you might not be able to understand what the figures of your income statement mean.

As long as you are in a position to understand your income statement, you should gain a lot of benefits from it. Some of the benefits of an income statement to the business owners and board of managers include:

1. Helps determine Net Sales (sales or revenue): The first important factor we can determine from the income sheet is the net sales value. The net sales of a company can help us learn a lot about the business. First, most investors and other interested parties will not associate with any business that is not making sales. The potential of a company to generate profit can be seen from its net sales. The net sales value will determine the ultimate profits of the company. Even if the products being sold have a very small profit margin, more sales will lead to more profits in the long run. Therefore, it is necessary to ensure that for all the income statements you review, the net sales value either grows, decreases, or

remains constant.

2. Cost of Sale (COGS): The other important factor we can determine from the income statement is the cost of goods sold. Unfortunately, it is sometimes difficult to determine the exact cost of goods sold before preparing the income sheet. In other words, a business might operate blindly for a long time. The longer a business operates blindly, the more likely the company will make losses. It is therefore important for all businesses to determine the cost of goods sold and use the value of goods sold to plan for the day to day operations of the company. A good accountant must provide the full range of the costs incurred in production. Some of the factors to consider under the costs of goods sold is the price for raw materials, labor, and manufacturing processes, among others.

3. Gross Profit: The other important information you can learn from the income statement is the gross profit and the gross margin. These two aspects are important in determining the overall profitability of your business operations. A business might have a slim net profit, yet it has a huge gross profit. It is only through the income sheet that you can determine the differences between the net profit and the gross profit. Such differences will help you make changes that will help reduce operational costs and increase the net

income of the business.

To determine the gross profit, we subtract the cost of goods sold from the gross revenue

Gross Profit = Gross revenue - COGS

4. General and Administrative Expenses: Although most people don't pay attention to operational expenses, they are very vital when it comes to determining the net profit of a company. Some operational expenses may make the cost of production too high, making it impossible for the company to make profits. Most financial analysts assume that management exercises a great deal of control over these expenses. In other words, the cost of operations can be increased or lowered, depending on the policies adopted by managers. If the company is struggling to earn an income, it is the duty of the managers to ensure that necessary operational expenses are cut down. If the company is already making sufficient profits, the company can use such income to make the working conditions better and even increase the productivity of the company. It is, therefore, necessary for you as the owner or manager of the business to look at the income sheet and use it to make informed decisions.

5. Operating Income: The other factor you can determine

from your income statement is the operating income. In other words, the operating income of a business refers to the income before interest and taxes. This figure gives you a clear picture of how the business generates its profits. If you are making an operating income that is substantial to cover all the operations and cost of goods sold, your business is in a good position. However, if your operating income cannot sustain the business operations, it will be much harder for the business to survive much longer.

Operating income = Gross Profit - Operating Expenses

The operating income mainly represents the earnings of the company before operating expenses such as interest, insurance, and taxes have been charged. This figure gives a true reflection of the company's position financially. The operating income is used as a measure of analysis and to determine the profitability of the company.

6. Interest Expense: The other important aspect you can learn from your income sheet is the state of your company's borrowing. Some companies have to pay too much interest on borrowed funds that they do not remain with any profits. Through the income sheet, you can determine the amount to be paid on borrowed money and determine whether the

interest being paid supports the continued operations of your business.

7. Pretax Income: The other important aspect you can determine from your income sheet is the earnings before tax. The earnings before tax help determine the amount of taxes to be paid. They also indicate the stability of the business and the ability of the business to sustain its operations. Earnings before taxes are determined by subtracting the sum of interest and operational costs from the gross profit.

Pretax Income = Gross Profit - (Interest + Operational costs)

As we have seen, operational costs can be adjusted to increase the profitability of the business. If you find that the profit of a company is being strained by interest and operational costs, you have the chance of adjusting operation costs to help cover up the interest and increase the net profits of the company.

8. Income Taxes: The income statement will help you calculate the income tax payable at the end of the trading period. Depending on the scale of your business, there is a percentage of your income that you are supposed to remit to the government as tax. For small businesses, about 30% of

the pretax income has to be remitted as taxes. From the income sheet, you can easily calculate the income tax payable in the ending trading period and submit your taxes to the relevant government authorities. Without the income statement, you may not know the amount required to be paid as taxes. Further, government agencies mandated with collecting income taxes may also want to prove the authenticity of the taxes you pay. In many instances, you will have auditors from the IRA check your books and to validate the information provided within the income statement.

9. Special Items or Extraordinary Expenses: The other important factor you can identify from your income sheet is the extraordinary expenses. At the end of the trading period, some expenses that are not regular in a business calendar may occur. For instance, if you end up writing off some of the assets of the company, there will be a loss of assets from the business without necessarily selling it. Such expenses must be accounted for when preparing the income statement. The income statement can, therefore, be used by the managers and owners to determine any expenses that are outside the scope of normal business operations.

10. Net Income: Most importantly, the income statement helps you determine the net income of the company. The net income refers to the income of the company after deducting

all expenses, including taxes. If the expenses can exceed the income of your business, you will end up with a net loss. After determining the net profit, you may now distribute the money accordingly. The net income is usually used to pay dividends to preferred shareholders. Any of the money that remains is invested back into the business as retained earnings. Without the income statement, it is not possible for you as the business owner to determine your earnings as an individual, the amounts of dividends to be paid to preferred shareholders, and the amount of money to be retained in the business. You need to look at your net income and the other aspects of your income sheet to know how the earnings of the business are being used.

11. Comprehensive Income: Last but not least, you can use your income statement to determine the comprehensive income of the business. However, the term comprehensive income is only used by large corporations that operate internationally. Comprehensive income is the net income of business adjusted for foreign currency exchange rates and minimum pension liability adjustments, among other factors. Although there are companies that provide comprehensive income figures on their income statement, most companies only offer the net income figures. The net income shows the value that best represents a company's earnings within the given period.

The income sheet is an important financial statement that can help any business owner make very important decisions. In most cases, the business owner and manager may have to ask some questions from the accountants just to get a clear picture of all the items depicted. If your accountant provides a summarized income sheet, demand to have a detailed income statement that comprises all the factors we have mentioned above.

Learning from the Statement of Owner's Equity

Besides the income statement, we have also prepared the statement of owner's equity. This is an important document that can be used to offer value to any business. In most cases, the statement of owner's equity is used by the owners of the business and interested investors. Investors who may be interested in purchasing the stock of a company may want to know about the portion of the business's assets that are acquired by loans. A business that has a lower debt to equity ratio is one that borrows less. In other words, it is a company that can finance its assets without necessarily depending on loans.

When it comes to analyzing and understanding the statement of owner's equity, you can use the ratios used to analyze the balance sheet. For instance, the equity to debt ratio determines the level of owner's equity compared to liabilities. At the same time, the statement of owner's equity can be used to determine whether a business is growing or declining. A business that is on an upward trend should continue increasing its portion of the owner's equity. However, if its owner's equity value starts falling, chances are that the business will end up having more debts than it can settle and consequently topple. There are many factors you can learn from the statement of owner's equity. Some of the important things you can learn from this statement include:

1. Return on capital invested: The first important lesson you should learn from your statement of retained earnings is the return earned on capital. For most people who get into the business, the aim is to make money and invest it into the business until it grows to a certain level. If you have been reinvesting earned capital into the business, chances are that you should see growth in the value of owners' capital. As we have already mentioned, the owner's capital represents the portion of the company that directly belongs to you as the owner. If you started the business as a partnership, it represents the portion of the company that is owned by the two partners. After several years of operations, you should see that the capital invested bring some returns. If the capital

is not bringing in returns, chances are that your business is on the decline, and it will end up falling short of your expectations.

2. The need for financing activities: The other important factor to consider is the need for financing. The value of the owner's equity versus the liabilities of a company can tell you whether you need to invest in or borrow more. If a company has more liabilities than the owner's equity, chances are that investing in the business as the owner is a better option as compared to borrowing. If a business has a higher owner's equity value than liabilities, it means that you can borrow from other lenders to facilitate the growth of your business. It is important to ensure that your equity to debt ratio does not go over 40%. For a stable business, equity to debt ratio should be relatively balanced. With that said, if your business can run well without the need to borrow, keep on managing it until it is absolutely necessary to bring in external sources of income.

3. The debt level of a company: The debt level of a company can also be determined by looking at the balance sheet, which gives us the value of the owner's equity. Even if you do not have access to the balance sheet, but you have access to your income sheet, you can determine the value of liabilities.

$$\text{Total Liability} = \text{Total Assets} - \text{Owner's Equity}$$

From this formula, you can easily determine the debt of the company and compare it to owners' equity. As we have already established, you should never borrow more than the company can sustain.

4. The level of retained earnings: Most importantly, the statement of owner's equity helps us determine the level of retained earnings. It is important that every business retains some earnings every year. If your business is making profits, but none is retained, it means that the business will not grow. As a matter of fact, a business that does not have retained earnings will have a declining owner's equity, which may lead to collapse any time soon.

$$\text{Owners' Equity} = \text{Starting Balance} + \text{Retained earnings}$$

From our explanation in the first chapter, the owner's equity is simply the capital invested by the owners at the start of the business. For example, assume that you wish to start a business with a capital of $10,000. Once you do your market survey and you are ready to start, you realize that to purchase the necessary tools and make your business operational, you will need $14000 and not the $10,000 you have at hand. To fund your business, you borrow $4000 from a bank in the name of the business. When you are starting this business, it will have a net worth of $14000.

Assuming that you use all the money you have to purchase the assets of the company, including the inventory and cash at hand, your total assets will be worth $14000. From our balance sheet equation

Assets = Liabilities + Owners Equity.

As you can see from our figures above, the total assets =$14000, the total liabilities =$4000; consequently, the owner's equity will be $10,000. In other words, the portion of the entire business owned by the proprietor of the enterprise is what we call owners' equity.

Now, it is important to remember that owner's equity can grow or decrease. There are two ways of growing the owner's equity. One way is by investing more cash or cash equivalents to the business. In the example above, if you choose to add $2000 to the business and only borrow $2000 from the bank, your owner's equity will consequently increase from $10000 to about $12000. The other way of increasing the owner's equity is by retaining part of the profits earned. Now, assuming that in the example above, you start the business at $14000, and it operates for one year, making a net profit of $3000. From this amount, you choose to spend $2000 and reinvest $1000 into the business. At the start of the next trading year, your owner's equity will have grown by $1000 to $11,000.

While the owner's equity of a business can grow from everyday business operations, it can also reduce from everyday business operations. The main cause of the reduction in the owner's equity is business losses and depreciation. If a business makes a loss of $1000 a year after you started operating, this value will be deducted from your equity. In other words, the value of the owner's equity will drop from $10,000 to about $9,000. Further, even if your business makes profits, but you don't retain any of the amounts in your business, chances are that your business will start depreciating. Assets lose their value as time goes by. If you had bought an asset worth $5000 at the start of the business, it might reduce its value to $3000 after 5 years of use. In case you do not retain any of your earnings, there will be no cash to purchase new assets, and in the long run, the business will not be able to continue operating.

Learning from the Statement of Cash Flow

Last but not least, there is a lot of information you can learn from the statement of cash flow. The statement of cash flow is similar to the income statement but not the same. The statement of cash flow simply shows where revenues are coming from and how the money of the business is being invested. As we have already seen, cash flow activities are categorized into operating, investing, and financing cash flows. From the statement of cash flows, you can learn the following.

1. Determine your net income: The first and most important lesson you can learn from your cash flow statement is the total revenue of the company and the sources of revenue. Although you can determine the total revenue of the business from your income statement, the figures provided by the cash flow statement are very comprehensive. The income sheet only shows revenue earned from operating activities and some investing activities. However, the cash flow statement offers a comprehensive analysis of all the sources of income, including investing and financing activities. While the income sheet may provide a detailed list of the company's expenditures, it does not show the impact of certain activities on your net profit. A look at the cash flow statement will help

you determine the impact of certain activities on your business. You will be able to determine how much the payment of loans and interest on loans affects your net income. In general, a look at the cash flow statement provides a holistic view of your income and the possible sources of income for the business.

2. Convert your net income from operating activities to net cash (flows): The cash flow statement also helps in converting the earnings from operating activities to cash. When we prepare the income statement, we do not care whether the cash being used has been disbursed or not. In most cases, we just prepare the income statement before the money is received by the business. This is because all businesses are required to use the accrual method of accounting. In the accrual method of accounting, all transactions are deemed complete once they take place and not when the money is paid. In other words, once you disburse goods to your clients, the transaction will be deemed complete even before you receive payment for the same goods. It is, therefore, necessary to find a way of balancing between the cash at hand and the cash receivable so that the continuous running of business activities does not come to a stop. It is only through the statement of cash flow that decisions can be made to ensure that there is a continuous flow of cash.

3. Given that the cash flow statement reflects a much realistic state of current cash affairs, it is used by managers of the business to facilitate day to day operations. For the statement of cash flows, you can regulate the rate at which you disburse cash out to suppliers. For instance, if you have supplied goods worth $5,000 to a customer, yet your supplier has provided raw materials worth $3000, you should be careful when distributing your money. Do not be quick to pay your supplier before your customers pay for their goods. The statement of cash flow shows the expenses happening, and the revenues being earned in real-time. In other words, you can use the value of all the revenue earned and the value of all the expenses undertaken to determine the amount of cash you will need to keep the business operating for a given duration. Without such prudent management of your income and expenses, you might be left without any cash to continue running your business at a crucial moment.

4. Calculate the net cash from investing activities and financing activities: The cash flow statement may also help you calculate the net cash from investing and financing activities. As we have seen, investing activities may include the purchase or sale of long-term assets. In such a case, you may spend heavily or earn large sums from investing activities. It is only through the statement of cash flows that

you can determine the net cash made from all the investing and financing activities. As we have already seen, the income statement only focuses on cash from operating activities. In other words, the income statement will give you the net cash from operating activities (net income). While the net income is an important component of a business, there are many other sources of income and expenditure that we must cater to in the running of the business. As we have already seen, if you do not retain any earnings in your business, the owner's equity value will keep on depreciating. In other words, this portion of a business cannot be taken care of by the profits earned unless you choose to invest the profits in the business.

The two areas of a business that are greatly affected and are not accounted for by the income sheet include the financing and the investing activities. To determine the net investing activities, you will have to subtract the negative investing activities from the positive investing activities.

In other words, if you purchase a new company van at $4000 and sell an old company van at $1000 in the same trading period, you will have to record the purchase as a negative investing activity. In other words, it is an activity that takes money from the company. You will also record the sale of a used van as a positive investing activity; in other words, it brings money into the business.

To determine the net investing activities, you will have to subtract the cost of purchasing the van from the money obtained from the sale of the van. In our example, we will end up with a negative $3000. This means that the company has spent $3000 on investments in this trading period. From the other cash flow activities, you must find the source of this money. Unless you can trace the source of the money used in investments, the business might not be sustainable in the long run.

Chapter 5: Precautions and Mistakes to Avoid

Now that we have looked at the various financial statements and how you can use each of the statements for your business, I want us to look at some mistakes you should avoid. In this final chapter, we will mainly focus on errors and mistakes that could be costly in accounting. As we have already seen, there are some mistakes that may lead to errors in ledger books or the trial balance. You should try avoiding such mistakes at all costs. After looking at the mistakes, we will crown up our book by looking at the basic principles you must keep in your mind, and the frequently asked questions by some accountants.

Mistakes Made by Amateur Accountants

If you are just starting to manage books of accounts, you should be cautious not to make some mistakes. Even if you are the owner of the business, it is important to keep track of all the transactions and get rid of stupid mistakes that may be costly at the end. Some of the expensive accounting mistakes that most people make include:

1. Failure to keep the accounts receivable: The most common mistake made by most people is that they avoid preparing the accounts receivable when dealing with the cash method of bookkeeping. Even if you will be dealing with the cash method of bookkeeping, it is important to maintain the accounts receivable. While small businesses such as sole proprietorships are allowed to use the cash method of bookkeeping, this does not eliminate the need for maintaining accounts receivable. Every business will have customers who purchase on credit. If you fail to maintain the accounts receivable, chances are that you will end up losing too much money due to failure in tracking down some cash.

2. Failure to track cash transactions: The other mistake is usually a failure to track cash transactions for those who use the accrual method of accounting. The accrual method of

accounting requires that all transactions be recorded as soon as they happen. In simple terms, money doesn't have to change hands before a transaction is deemed complete. The downside of this method of accounting is that most accountants tend to focus on large significant transactions such as the purchase of raw materials, etc. If you fail to keep track of the smaller transactions that happen along the way, you may end up losing money through smaller transactions that pile up in the long run. For this reason, it is important for all businesses to maintain a petty cash book, which caters to the seller transactions. Such transactions mainly include operational costs that may pile up in the long run if precautions are not taken.

3. Poor communication between the accountant and bookkeeper: The other common mistake that happens in most companies is a lack of communication between the accountant and the bookkeeper. As already mentioned in our first chapter, the duties of an accountant and bookkeeper are complimentary. The accountant cannot do proper accounting unless he/she receives the right data from the bookkeeper. On the other hand, a bookkeeper may not offer any value unless the data recorded is used by an accountant. It is, therefore, necessary to have regular communication between the two parties. The accountant must supervise the work done by the bookkeeper and provide guidance. If you

choose to carry out bookkeeping yourself, make sure you bring in an accountant from time to time just to ensure that the quality of your records is up to date with accounting standards.

4. Using improper or outdated bookkeeping software: The other common accounting mistake made by most accountants is using improper accounting software. The accounting software used will determine the quality of records that are kept. Today, most companies use automated accounting software. The automation helps in recording transactions in real-time to reduce the chances of fraud. However, you should never use any software without knowing how it works. If you wish to introduce new accounting software, it is recommended that you bring on board an experienced accountant to help guide the other staff on using it. This way, you get to use new tools that will ensure accuracy in all the work you do.

5. Failure to keep documents that prove the occurrence of transactions: Accounts are most often audited by government agencies or internal auditors. The work of auditing helps determine whether the bookkeeping and accounting methods are straightforward. In some instances, people may use fraudulent means of accounting to ensure that the books balance. The only way to prove the

authenticity of all transactions is by keeping the documents. There are many documents that are used to prove that a transaction has occurred. For instance, you will need a bank slip to prove that cash was deposited or withdrawn over the counter. You may need a copy of the check to prove that payment has been made. You may need a receipt to prove that a certain item has been purchased. It is important to file and digitize all documents that prove the occurrence of transactions. If you digitize such documents, you can store them in multiple media and easily retrieve them if need be. Such documents are important since they are needed when you start tracking down errors. Errors made in the subsidiary books of entry can only be found and corrected from the source documents.

6. Failure to consolidate subsidiary books with the general ledger: The other common mistake that amateur accountants make is a failure to consolidate the subsidiary books of entry with the general ledger. If you take too long to summarize the subsidiary book entries, they may pile up and become challenging to consolidate. When you have recorded the important entries in the subsidiary books, you should add up all the summaries and transfer them to the general ledger. When transferring, make sure you double-check with the source documents so that you do not end up transferring errors from one book to another.

7. Failure to prepare the trial balance: Lastly, most people who are new to accounting may jump into preparing financial statements without preparing the trial balance. As we have already seen, although the trial balance is not one of the financial statements, it is deemed as one of the most important tools in understanding the financial position of a business. From the trial balance, we can validate the authenticity of the general ledger entries. It is important to double-check such entries to ensure that the final records presented through the financial statements reflect the true status of a company. If you end up preparing financial statements with plenty of errors, you may end up paying more taxes than you should.

Accounting Basics You Should Never Forget

There are some accounting basics you should never forget. These basics determine the ability of an accountant to provide accurate financial statements. If you are the owner or manager of a business, you must also keep such basics at the back of your mind to help you in decision making. Some of the accounting basics to keep at the mind include

1. Accounting software is as important as the accountant: The most important thing about bookkeeping

and accounting is having the right software. Even if you have the best bookkeeper or accountant in the world, they may not be able to perform unless you provide the right software. Accounting software is particularly important when dealing with bookkeeping. Most businesses have automated transaction recording software that helps track down all the transactions that occur within the business. When you purchase bookkeeping and accounting software, find one that can be used by all employees while at the same time providing the ultimate security to the financial management departments.

2. Cash flow tracking is the backbone: As soon as you start operating your business, set up your business bank account. One mistake that most people make when getting into business is using one account for business and personal finances. The best way to manage your business is by maintaining a bank account that helps you control all your cash flows. When managing your cash flow, you should watch the timing of the money coming and going out. Through prudent management of cash, you will be able to plan for your future investments, run the day-to-day operations, and determine your profits without a problem.

3. Keep track of your inventory: The biggest problem that most people have to face is getting the actual count of

inventory. Accounting for inventory becomes even more difficult when you offer services rather than goods. When accounting for inventory, make sure you include both direct and indirect costs. Account for the cost of all materials, any costs of packaging the products, and make a decision about the volume of inventory you wish to have at hand.

4. Understand your cost of goods sold: The other basic factor you must keep in mind when it comes to accounting is the cost of goods sold. If you do not determine the accurate cost of goods sold, chances are that you may end up making losses. The cost of goods sold determines the price of the products you sell and, consequently, the profits you make. To determine the cost of goods sold, you will have to calculate based on the business model you are operating. For business models that involve production, you must include the cost of raw materials, the cost of labor, power, and other components used in production.

5. Get your expenses right: Besides the cost of goods sold, there are other expenses that a business has to undertake. The other expenses may be less than the cost of goods sold. However, there are some business models where operating expenses can easily match up to the cost of goods sold. Start by determining the fixed expenses of the business. These are business expenses that are constant, whether your business

is operational or not. Such expenses and indirect expenses will determine the overall profit of the business.

6. Figure out your break-even sales requirement: The other important factor to keep in mind is the break-even sales requirements. After determining the cost of goods sold and other expenses, it is your duty to determine the best pricing and the required sales volumes to meet all your expenses. If you fail to meet your break-even sales volume, your business will end up making losses. For all businesses, there is a level of production and sales that lead to profitability. You must target the sales that lead to profitability in the long run.

7. Track your sales and profits before tax: The other basic principle of accounting for managers is tracking of revenue and profits. If you can determine your revenue and expenses, you should be in a position to track your profits. By tracking your expenses and revenue, you can determine the possibility of your business making profits or losses even before we come to the end of the trading period.

8. Set up the proper tax rates for customers: As the business owner, you should implement managerial policies that provide room for the business to grow. When you want to set the prices and taxes for products and services, you must use accounting data. At the end of the day, financial statements

should not only help you make informed decisions but should also establish the best rates for customers. If the company is already making losses, looking at the cost of production, revenues, and other expenses, can help determine the right process to sell your goods to make profits.

9. Plan for your tax payments: Financial statements are meant to help you plan to pay your taxes at the right time. Understanding your earnings and expenses should help you make the right tax payment decisions. The taxes paid by a business depend on the profits earned and the physical location of the business. Governments have different tax requirements that must be met for your business to continue operating. One of the most basic needs of accounting is to determine the profits and, consequently, the tax payable during a given trading period.

10. Understand your balance sheet: Most importantly, it is necessary for any business owner or manager to understand the balance sheet. The balance sheet is the financial statement that shows the net worth of a business. Just by looking at the balance sheet, you can determine how much assets the business owns, the level of debts, and the value of the owner's equity. If you wish to establish your business well for future growth, you should be able to interpret your

balance sheet and use it accordingly.

How to Detect Accounting Problems from Financial Statements

As the owner or manager of a business, your main aim of reviewing financial statements is to ensure that they are accurate. When you look at financial statements, you should be able to tell whether the information provided is true or false. If you don't know how to review financial statements, you may end up making losses even if the business is profitable. When reviewing financial records, there are some ways you can detect errors. Here are some of the pointers to look out for to avoid using misleading financial statements.

1. Exclusion of financial transactions: Any prudent business manager will not only focus on financial statements but also review the ledger book and other books of entry. As a matter of fact, all financial statements can be manipulated to give a false image of the operations of a business. For instance, an accountant can choose to eliminate certain transactions completely. In such a case, the business might end up making losses without the owner or the manager noticing discrepancies. To ensure that you track all the errors that might occur, you should take a day or two just to review the other financial records. Go through the general ledger and

the subsidiary books of entry to determine any errors. If the accountants have left any transactions out, you can detect by looking at the source documents and comparing the transactions to those recorded in the general ledger.

2. Lack of correlation to previous financial statements: You should start asking questions if the financial statements prepared in consecutive accounting periods are completely unrelated. For instance, if the financial records for the trading period ending December 31st, 2019 are completely different from those prepared in June 2019, chances are that the figures are being cooked. If the figures are being cooked, the accountants may not be keen enough to maintain consistency throughout all the financial statements. You can look at the financial statements and compare them to those from previous trading periods to see if there are any discrepancies. For financial statements such as the income statement, it is okay to have significant variations. However, six months is not enough time to cause significant changes to the balance sheet or the owner's equity.

3. Lack of source documents to prove transactions: The other way to determine possible errors in your financial statement is by looking at source documents. One of the best indicators of the accuracy of your records is the cash and bank accounts. The cash account will help you determine all the

transactions that have happened throughout the trading period. For all the cash account transactions, you should be able to find the supporting documents. At the same time, the bank account can also help you determine the authenticity of transactions. Source documents such as bank slips and checks are important in proving that certain transactions took place over the trading period in question. Whenever you receive financial statements from your accountant, just pick one account and request for source documents regarding transactions in that account. For instance, you could ask for all transactions regarding cash going in and out of the bank. From such transactions, you will determine whether the figures provided on your income statement or the balance sheet are true.

4. Financial statements don't reflect reality: Besides proving the authenticity of the statements by looking at source documents, you should also use your best judgment. By best judgment, I mean you should be able to gauge the average income of the business based on the day to day activities of the business. For instance, if your business spends a lot of money on production and you happen to make a lot of sales, you should expect that your business brings in substantial revenue. However, if you realize that the value of goods sold or the accounts receivable is way higher as compared to the revenue, you must investigate the reasons behind such

discrepancies. In some cases, the accountants may make adjustments to the true figures of your accounts and siphon money out of your business if you don't make a critical analysis of the financial statements.

5. Analyze financial ratios: The other way to find out if there are errors in your financial records is by analyzing financial ratios. For instance, we have seen that the debt to equity ratio can be used to determine the stability of a business. If you happen to produce such ratios for each trading period, it will be easy for you to spot errors in your financial statements. If the ratios from the previous trading periods vary greatly, chances are that your accountants are using unscrupulous methods to siphon money out of the business. For instance, if you realize that your debt to equity ratio has increased yet you have not borrowed more, you are probably losing money to the accountants. The accountants can mess up with your owner's equity or the value of liabilities to find a way of stealing from the business. While the other figures on the financial statements may have significant differences as compared to the subsequent accounting period, financial ratios do not change much.

6. Hire an Internal Auditor: Last and most importantly, you must be ready to bring an internal auditor to look at the financial statements once they are prepared. Financial

auditors are professional accountants who specialize in auditing financial records and are better placed to fix errors made by other accountants. In accounting, errors can occur whether made intentionally or by mistake. Unfortunately, with errors of omission, the balance sheet and the trial balance will still balance well. Relying on documents such as the trial balance or the balance sheet to determine the accuracy of your financial records is not the best approach. These documents can only help you prove a few facts but will not show some serious errors. For this reason, you must find a way of reviewing the books of subsidiary entries. Have an auditor go through all the books of original entries and confirm the entries with the source documents. While hiring an accountant to audit your books might be the best way for those who lack accounting skills, you should be careful who you choose to trust. Some auditors may collude with accountants to steal from the company. You must make sure all the important source documents are available to help provide the best results for your audits.

FAQs about Financial Statements

At this stage, we have covered all the information you need to know about financial statements. You should be able to prepare and analyze financial statements without a problem. At the same time, you should be in a position to determine the errors within the financial statements.

What are the 5 elements of financial statements?

There are three key financial statements that are made up of 5 main elements. These elements include:

1. Assets: Assets are items of value that are owned by the company. Items that can be listed under assets include cash, equipment, real estate, etc.

2. Liabilities: These are items that decrease the net worth of the business. In other words, liabilities are what the company owes other companies, individuals, or investors. Liabilities include items such as accounts payable, long term and short term loans, etc.

3. Equities: These refer to cash or cash equivalents that are used to represent the ownership of the company. The term equity, as used in accounting, determines the value of the company and its ownership.

4. Revenues: Revenue is one component of financial statements that mainly appears on the income sheet and the cash flow statement. Revenue represents all the money that is earned by a business over a given trading period. The revenue of a business can vary from one accounting period to

another. The revenue of a business determines the net income of business after expenses have subtracted.

5. Expenses: The expenses of a business are usually used in preparing the income sheet and the cash flow statement. Expenses represent the ways a company uses its funds. Among the expenses include direct expenses such as the cost of goods sold and indirect expenses such as rent and taxes.

How do owners and managers use financial statements?

The owners of a business and managers are the main beneficiaries of financial statements. Although most people think financial statements are prepared for external investors and tax authorities, the truth is that business managers and owners need the statements more. Financial statements are used by managers to plan on the cost of production and reduce expenses. This way, managers are able to reduce operating expenses to increase the net income of a business. The board of managers also use the financial statements to determine the net worth of the business, the debt level, and the assets of the company. From the balance sheet, the managers can determine whether the business is in a position to borrow more to finance its activities.

Who is responsible for preparing financial statements?

The accounting office is responsible for preparing financial statements. Within the accounting office, we have accountants and bookkeepers. The work of bookkeepers is mainly recording transactions and preparing auxiliary statements such as the trial balance. The work of accountants is mainly preparing financial statements and interpreting them. However, there are companies that only hire an accountant without bookkeepers. In such a case, the accountant performs the duties of a bookkeeper.

What are the three main financial statements?

There are 3 main financial statements; the balance sheet, income statement, and cash flow statement.

1. The balance sheet: This is the financial statement that provides a snapshot of a company's net worth at a given point in time. The balance sheet mainly lists the assets, liabilities, and owner's equity. From the balance sheet, you can determine the net worth of the company and the debts of the business.

2. Income statement: The income statement is the other

important financial statement. It shows the income and expenses of a company. From the income statement, you can determine various sources of income and expenditure. You can also determine the net profit or net loss of the business.

3. The cash flow statement: Third most important financial statement is the cash flow statement. It shows the sources of money for business and how the money of the business is spent. The cash flow statement is used to determine the liquidity of a company and the possibility of the business to sustain its operations.

Which financial statement is most important to management?

All the three financial statements mentioned above are very important to the management. However, if I were to choose one as a business manager, I would go with the income statement. The balance sheet and the cash flow statements are important, but they can't match the value of the income statement. The income statement provides a true picture of the current operations of a business. From the income statement, you can determine where to invest and how to improve the income of the business. You can also find ways of cutting down expenditure to make the business more profitable.

What do investors use financial statements for?

Besides managers and owners of the business, financial statements are also very important to the owners of the business. External investors can use financial statements to determine whether a company is a possible investment partner. For instance, suppliers need to look at the statement of cash flows before they supply goods to a business. If a company has sufficient amounts of money in circulation, investors are confident that it can pay its debts. Investors also have to look at the balance sheet to determine if the company has a future. A company that has a future should have more assets and fewer debts. From the balance sheet, investors can determine the stability of the business financially.

Can bookkeepers prepare financial statements?

As already mentioned, the work of accounting is done by bookkeepers and accountants. However, the bookkeeper cannot handle the duties of an accountant. One of the important duties of an accountant is to prepare financial statements. The bookkeeper cannot prepare financial statements since bookkeepers are not certified, accountants. However, an accountant can perform all the duties of a bookkeeper, including recording transactions.

Conclusion

Congratulations on reading this book to the end. If you are interested in accounting in any way, you have gained valuable information that will help you perform your duties well. If you are a business manager, owner, or just an individual who wishes to know more about accounting, this book covers every bit of information you need. After reading the book, I will recommend going through it one more time with more focus on the section on preparing financial statements. Even if your intention is to interpret financial statements, you should try looking at the sections about preparing financial statements. If you can master preparing the statements, you will not have any problem interpreting yours.

To help you understand financial statements and even prepare them, we have simplified this book. You should not expect technical accounting terms or calculations within the book. The book breaks accounting in simple small chunks that are easy to understand for all. We mainly focus on basic accounting tools and financial statements. This book develops the subject of financial statements from the known and builds up to the unknown.

In this book, we have covered four main sections. The introductory section mainly focuses on new terms you will encounter in the book. To help you understand the book well, we look at some accounting terms and explain them in the simplest way possible. Further, we look at the benefits of financial statements and accounting as a whole. We help you understand the difference between accounting and bookkeeping and also understand the reasons why you should invest in accounting.

In the second section of the book, we introduce you to financial statements. Before you start preparing any financial statements, you should know what they are. The book gives you a snippet of each of the important financial statements. We have a look at what each financial statement is used for and how important it is to the business. We also have a look at the general use of each financial statement and help you understand the benefits of each statement to your business.

In the third section of the book, we focus on the preparation and analysis of financial statements. This section forms the core of the book and provides a detailed look at how financial statements are arrived at. For each of the financial statements, we provide the easiest ways of preparation and analysis. We introduce you to financial ratios that are used to analyze financial statements too.

Lastly, we look at the mistakes that could occur in accounting. As a manager or the owner of a business, you should always be on the lookout to avoid making mistakes. You should also be keen to detect any errors that may occur within financial statements. In the last section of the book, we look at some precautions you could take to seal loopholes. Most accountants and bookkeepers look for loopholes to steal the resources of the business. You must put in place regulations that can control leakage of company resources. We look at the ways you can spot errors within financial statements and try to resolve them before they develop into a full-blown financial crisis.

If you are a business owner or manager, this book will help you handle your duties effectively. This book may also be used by accounting students who wish to sharpen their practical accounting skills. From the start to the end, we use a practical approach to elaborating on every aspect of financial statements. We have used examples, images, and screenshots to help you conceptualize how all the statements are prepared.

Made in United States
Troutdale, OR
10/11/2024

23652081R00076